5.9/0.5
75724

Valley Forge

by Michael Burgan

Content Adviser: Julie Richter, Ph.D.,
Independent Scholar and Consultant,
Colonial Williamsburg Foundation

Reading Adviser: Dr. Linda D. Labbo,
Department of Reading Education, College of Education,
The University of Georgia

COMPASS POINT BOOKS
MINNEAPOLIS, MINNESOTA

Compass Point Books
3109 West 50th Street, #115
Minneapolis, MN 55410

Visit Compass Point Books on the Internet at *www.compasspointbooks.com*
or e-mail your request to *custserv@compasspointbooks.com*

On the cover: "Washington at Valley Forge" by E. Percy Morgan

Photographs ©: Library of Congress, cover, 14, 17, 21, 36; Rick Reeves, 4; Stock Montage, 5, 15; Courtesy West Chester University, where this portrait hangs in Tanglewood, the residence of the university president, 7; National Park Service/Harpers Ferry Center Commissioned Art Collection/artist Don Troiani, 8, 13, 26; Hulton/Archive by Getty Images, 9, 30, 39, 40; Richard Cummins/Corbis, 10; Lombard Antiquarian Maps & Prints, 11, 33; Kean Collection/Getty Images, 19, 27; Independence National Historical Park, 22, 28, 31, 34, 37; DVIC/NARA, 23; Bettmann/Corbis, 25; N. Carter/North Wind Picture Archives, 29, 35, 41.

Editor: Catherine Neitge
Photo Researcher: Svetlana Zhurkina
Designer/Page Production: Bradfordesign, Inc./Biner Design
Cartographer: XNR Productions, Inc.

Library of Congress Cataloging-in-Publication Data
Burgan, Michael.
   Valley Forge / by Michael Burgan.
      p. cm. — (We the people)
      Includes bibliographical references and index.
Contents: A hard winter—Losses on the field—Plans for the winter—Starvation and other troubles—Slow improvements—Moving out.
   ISBN 0-7565-0615-8
   1. Washington, George, 1732-1799—Headquarters—Pennsylvania—Valley Forge—Juvenile literature. 2. Valley Forge (Pa.)—History—18th century—Juvenile literature. 3. United States. Continental Army—History—Juvenile literature. 4. Pennsylvania—History—Revolution, 1775-1783—Juvenile literature. 5. United States—History—Revolution, 1775-1783—Juvenile literature. [1. United States—History—Revolution, 1775-1783—Campaigns. 2. Washington, George, 1732-1799. 3. Valley Forge (Pa.)—History—18th century.] I. Title. II. Series: We the people (Compass Point Books)
   E234.B927 2004
   973.3'341—dc22   2003014443

TABLE OF CONTENTS

A Hard Winter 4

Losses on the Field 8

Plans for the Winter 15

Starvation and Other Troubles 22

Slow Improvements 29

Moving Out 35

Glossary 42

Did You Know? 43

Important Dates 44

Important People 45

Want to Know More? 46

Index 48

NOTE: *In this book, words that are defined in the glossary are in* **bold** *the first time they appear in the text.*

A HARD WINTER

At the end of 1777, General George Washington and his men set up camp at Valley Forge, Pennsylvania. The general commanded the Continental Army, the force

4

General George Washington inspects the troops at Valley Forge.

American troops suffered through a cold winter at Valley Forge.

trying to win American independence from Great Britain. At Valley Forge, Washington faced many problems. His troops had struggled during the year. British forces had recently captured Philadelphia, the first capital of the United States. Washington also had trouble finding enough supplies, clothes, and shoes for his army of about 12,000 men and boys.

At Valley Forge, many American soldiers often went barefoot. For a time, they slept in tents that barely kept out the winter cold. Disease spread through the camp, and food was sometimes scarce. Just before Christmas, Washington wrote, "There is not a single [animal] of any kind to slaughter and less than 25 barrels of flour! We do not know when to expect more."

By the spring, however, the situation at Valley Forge began to change. Congress improved the system for delivering food and other supplies. As the weather warmed, the men trained harder than ever to improve their skills. A Prussian officer, Friedrich von Steuben, led this effort. In April 1778, the United States also received good news from France. The French were joining the war against Great Britain.

By June 1778, Washington was ready to take on the British again. His army was larger and better trained for battle. The war would last for another three years, but the United States had strengthened itself during the hard winter at Valley Forge. The name Valley Forge would always stand for the Americans' deep desire to fight for independence, no matter how hard the struggle.

A portrait of George Washington by famous painter Charles Willson Peale

LOSSES ON THE FIELD

Fighting the American Revolution was never easy for General Washington. He often struggled to put enough soldiers in the field. By the summer of 1777, the general had about 12,000 troops under his command. They included members of the Continental Army and different state **militias.** At the same time, the British had about 18,000 troops nearby.

That summer, General Washington spent much of his time wondering where

A soldier in the Continental Army

the British would attack. Their commander, Sir William Howe, had taken his troops out of New Jersey and moved them to New York. Howe's plan was to bring about 15,000 troops into Pennsylvania by ship. His goal was to capture

Sir William Howe was commander in chief of British forces in North America.

Philadelphia and destroy the American force.

In late August, the British landed in Maryland, then moved through Delaware into Pennsylvania. On September 11, the Americans fought the British along Brandywine Creek, about 25 miles (40 kilometers) west of Philadelphia.

x

General Washington's headquarters at Brandywine

General Washington did not know the land in the area. He also received bad **intelligence** from one of his officers. The British won the Battle of Brandywine, forcing Washington to retreat. As one American soldier later wrote, "Our army was something broke." A few weeks later, the British marched into Philadelphia.

On October 4, Washington launched a surprise attack on the British. Howe's main army was camped outside of Philadelphia, at Germantown. The Americans attacked them through a thick fog, and at first Washington's men

The Battle of Germantown

11

seemed to be in control. As the battle went on, however, the Americans could not see through the fog. Some soldiers fired at their own troops. Many also wasted time and **ammunition** trying to take a small stone house filled with British troops. The Americans soon retreated. In the end, the Continental Army had more **casualties** than the British. Neither side could claim a clear victory. Washington called Germantown "unfortunate," but not a major setback.

For a time, Washington considered trying another direct attack. Already, however, he was facing supply problems. In Congress, two different departments played a role in supplying the army. The **Commissary** Department actually bought the troops' supplies. The **Quartermaster** Department then made sure the supplies reached the soldiers in the field. During the summer, the leaders of these departments had quit. The new leaders of the Commissary Department did not have experience buying supplies for thousands of troops. In the meantime, Congress delayed in finding a new quartermaster general, the head of the Quartermaster Department.

To help supply the troops, the Pennsylvania government called out its militia. The local soldiers took weapons, clothing, and blankets from anyone who had supported the British

A Continental soldier loads his musket.

or refused to help the Americans. At the same time, the British continued to attack. Their targets were two American forts that protected the Delaware River. To reach Philadelphia, British ships had to sail past Fort Mifflin and Fort Mercer. By the end of November, Howe's troops had forced the Americans to leave both forts.

An illustration from an 1859 book shows the Americans fighting the British at Fort Mifflin on the Delaware River.

PLANS FOR THE WINTER

During November, Washington kept his troops at Whitemarsh, just north of Philadelphia. The army grew as more soldiers arrived from New York. There, at the Battle of Saratoga, the Americans had won a major

British General John Burgoyne surrendered to American General Horatio Gates after the Battle of Saratoga.

victory. The U.S. commander at the battle, Horatio Gates, was praised as a hero. Afterward, some members of Congress began to think that Gates, not Washington, should command all the U.S. troops.

Washington's troubles seemed to grow along with the size of his army. In addition to the supply problems, he had to deal with the approaching winter. He also faced disagreements between the political leaders and his own staff.

During the late 18th century, armies usually did not fight during the winter. They found a safe place to set up camp or sent soldiers to live in nearby villages. The Americans, however, had used a different strategy during the previous winter. In late December 1776 and January 1777, Washington had fought and won several key battles in New Jersey, including battles at Trenton and Princeton. At the end of 1777, some U.S. leaders wanted him to stay "in the field" again. The Americans

Washington and his troops crossed the Delaware River in December 1776 before surprising the British at the Battle of Trenton.

would remain close to Philadelphia and fight the British when they had the chance.

Within the army, however, most of Washington's officers opposed staying in the field. They believed keeping the men safe and healthy was the most important goal.

17

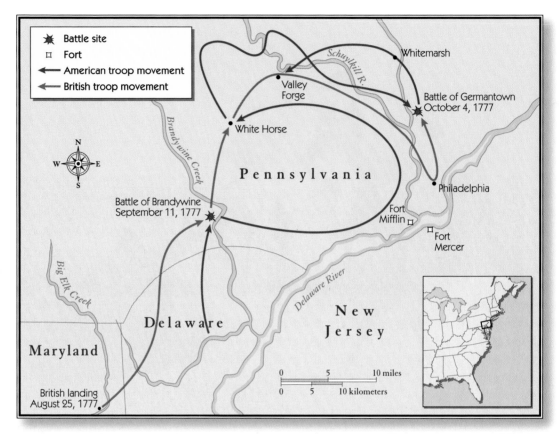

Troop movements and battles

That way, the army would be ready for battle in the spring. Some of the officers called for pulling back into Delaware. Others wanted to move farther west into Pennsylvania. A few suggested staying closer to Philadelphia and building huts to shelter the men through the winter.

In mid-December, Washington made his decision. The army began to move west, across the Schuylkill River. The men would set up camp in huts near towns to protect American **civilians** from any British attack. When

Continental Army troops make their way to Valley Forge.

19

Washington announced his plan, he told the troops he would "share in the hardship and…inconvenience" they faced during the long winter.

On December 19, Washington and his army reached their winter campsite—Valley Forge. The spot was named for the iron **forges** in the area. Also close by were many farms that produced different types of grain. The area between Valley Forge and Philadelphia also had many dairy farms and orchards. The region did not have a shortage of food, since that year's harvest had been good. The problem Washington faced was getting enough of that food to his troops.

The move to Valley Forge cut off the supply lines Washington had developed at Whitemarsh. Now he had to find new sources of food for his army. His men also had to build the wooden huts that would shelter them through the winter. In addition, Washington had military concerns. His men had to patrol the region, looking

George Washington faced many problems at Valley Forge.

for enemy activity. At times, the British left Philadelphia
to search for food. The Americans wanted to prevent
these efforts.

21

STARVATION AND OTHER TROUBLES

Just after arriving at Valley Forge, Washington learned that the British were sending a large force into the Pennsylvania countryside. The general wanted to send troops after them. Some of his officers, however, said the lack of food and supplies made that impossible. One general, James Varnum, told

A portrait of General James Varnum by Charles Willson Peale

Washington that his troops had not eaten in three days. He and another officer feared that the men might revolt as they faced starvation. "The men must be supplied," Varnum said, "or they cannot be commanded." Another officer said the men might start robbing nearby civilians if food did not arrive soon.

On December 22, 1777, Washington wrote to Congress and explained his situation. In addition to the shortage of food, almost 3,000 men lacked shoes or clothing and could

George Washington met with members of Congress at Valley Forge.

not fight. Washington asked, "What then is to become of the army this winter?" He believed it would either starve or break apart if the supply problem was not solved. Some historians say the general may have exaggerated his fears. He wanted Congress to know how deep the problem was, however, and made sure they fixed it quickly.

Despite the lack of food, some American forces were able to go after the British on their **foraging** missions. The Americans ended up finding food for themselves, too. Slowly, the supply lines began to work again, and more food reached Valley Forge. Still, in early January, a colonel from Massachusetts described an army that was "bad enough." The colonel wrote to a friend, "To see our poor brave fellows living in tents, bare-footed, bare-legged…in snow, in rain, on marches, in camp, and on duty, without being able to supply their wants is really distressing." The colonel also noted that large supplies of provisions were finally reaching the camp from New England.

General Washington visits wounded soldiers at Valley Forge.

Congress finally started to take action. The lawmakers were now based in York, west of Valley Forge.
Washington's letter of December 22 had convinced
Congress it had to act. First, it ordered extra pay for the
soldiers at Valley Forge. More money was offered to
officers who gave their usual extra food **rations** to the
men. The lawmakers then began studying how to

Two officers of the Continental Army

improve supplying the troops. They also considered
Washington's request to improve the overall organization
of the army.

At times, Washington felt Congress was as much of
a problem as the British. The lawmakers tried to manage
all the military efforts, instead of letting him make deci-
sions. Washington also believed that Congress thought

26

too highly of foreign officers who were helping the Americans. These officers sometimes received promotions, while American officers were passed over. One of these foreign-born officers was Thomas Conway of Ireland. He had fought with Washington in Pennsylvania, and the general was not impressed with his skills. Still, Congress promoted

General Washington greets a soldier at Valley Forge.

27

Conway to the position of inspector general. He was sup-
posed to help train the troops at Valley Forge and report to
Congress on Washington's actions.

Washington also knew that some members of Congress
blamed him for the recent losses in Pennsylvania. Some
wanted to replace him as commander in chief. Even before
the army reached Valley Forge,
Washington suspected that these
congressmen wanted to make
Horatio Gates the commander
in chief. Congress did name
Gates to the Board of War.
Some members of Congress
wanted to use this board to
command the army. In the
end, however, Washington had
enough support in Congress to
keep his position as commander.

A portrait of General Horatio Gates
by Charles Willson Peale

SLOW IMPROVEMENTS

By the end of January, the men at Valley Forge were out of their tents and living in huts. Despite the earlier grumbling, most of the troops accepted the harsh conditions they faced. One officer wrote, "Every hardship and distress, they have

Cabins like those used by Continental soldiers have been reconstructed at Valley Forge.

29

encountered and endured without…complaint." The next month, however, the supply lines broke down again, and the situation grew worse. At the same time, the weather turned cold and wet. Some of the soldiers **deserted,** while a few officers tried to resign.

By His EXCELLENCY
SIR WILLIAM HOWE, K. B.
General and Commander in Chief, &c. &c. &c.
PROCLAMATION.

WHEREAS by my Declaration dated the 27th of August, 1777, Security and Protection were promised to all Perfons, Inhabitants of Pennfylvania, &c. &c. &c. excepting only thofe, who have affumed legiflative or judicial Authority, provided they did forthwith return, and remain peaceably at their ufual Places of Abode.

THIS is to make known to all Perfons, who, in Confequence of the faid Declaration, have complied with the fame, that they may rely upon a due Confideration being hereafter fhewn to them provided they do not forfeit their Pretenfions by a future Conduct.—And further to Proclaim, that thofe only who have availed themfelves before this Date of the Indulgences fet forth in my faid Declaration, fhall be efteemed entitled to the Benefits thereof.

Given under my Hand at Head-quarters, near Germantown, the 28th day of September, 1777.

W. HOWE.

By his Excellency's Command,

ROBERT MACKENZIE. Sec'ry.

Philadelphia; Printed by James Humphreys, junr.

A proclamation by Sir William Howe promised to protect Pennsylvanians who sided with the British.

To end the food shortage, Washington ordered supplies sent from camps in neighboring states. He also sent out several thousand troops on a foraging mission. In the field, U.S. troops tried to prevent civilians from selling food to the British. Many Pennsylvanians—

as well as residents of other states—supported the British. These "Loyalists" preferred selling their products to the British instead of the Continental Army. Some citizens sold to the British for another reason. The British money they received was more valuable than the money issued by the U.S. government.

Despite the second severe food shortage, once again Washington was able to keep his army together. And once again, the supply lines strengthened. The supply crisis improved even more in March. That month, Congress made General Nathanael Greene quartermaster general as well as head of the Commissary

A portrait of Nathanael Greene by Charles Willson Peale

Department. (Congress later put Jeremiah Wadsworth in charge of the Commissary Department.) Greene worked hard to make sure Washington had enough supplies through the spring. The quartermaster general improved relations with the civilians of the region by paying them promptly when he bought goods.

Another major change came in March, as the American troops began to train in a new way. In February, Friedrich von Steuben arrived at Valley Forge. He called himself a baron—a member of a royal family. In reality, Steuben was not a baron. He was a skilled officer, however, willing to help the Americans. Steuben had fought for his homeland of Prussia. This German-speaking European nation was famous for its professional, skilled troops. Steuben planned to use Prussian training methods to make the Americans better soldiers.

Steuben did not speak English, but he did speak French. An American officer who knew French translated for Steuben when he met Washington. The Prussian

Friedrich von Steuben used Prussian methods to train American soldiers.

impressed Washington. The commander called him "a gentleman, and as far as I have had an opportunity to judge, a man of military knowledge."

33

Steuben was amazed when he saw the American troops for the first time. He could not believe the tattered clothes they wore to fight off the cold. He also noted, "With regard to their military discipline I can safely say no such thing existed." Steuben's first job was writing a book that outlined the drills that the soldiers should practice. These

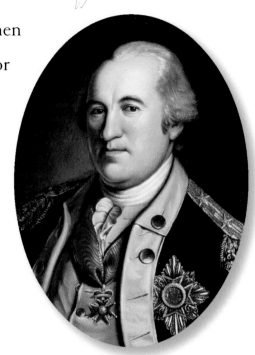

A portrait of Friedrich von Steuben by Charles Willson Peale

drills would improve their skills as soldiers. Next, he took 120 of the best Continental troops and taught them the drills. The men learned how to follow orders for marching and quickly firing their weapons. After two weeks of training, these soldiers then taught their new skills to the other Americans at Valley Forge. Slowly, all the troops learned the new methods for fighting.

MOVING OUT

As spring approached, the mood in the camp began to improve. The weather slowly warmed, and the supply problems began to fade. Under Steuben's direction, the Continental Army became a better fighting force. Best of all, Washington and his men learned that foreign help was on the way. France had decided to join the war against Great Britain.

Washington's headquarters at Valley Forge

35

Washington and Lafayette inspect the camp at Valley Forge.

France had already been sending supplies to the
Americans. Some French had also volunteered to fight for
American independence. The most notable was the

Marquis de Lafayette. This French **nobleman** had fought under Washington during 1777 and spent the harsh winter at Valley Forge. Now, the French were willing to send ships and thousands of soldiers to fight the British.

Although the situation had improved, everything was not perfect at Valley Forge. By early May, the army had grown to about 13,000 troops ready for battle. The increasing number of troops once again caused a shortage of food, especially beef. This time, however, the shortage ended quickly, and Washington was ready to send a large force into the field.

The commander ordered Lafayette to take about 2,500 men to Barren Hill. This location was about halfway between

A portrait of the Marquis de Lafayette by Charles Willson Peale

Valley Forge and Philadelphia. Washington wanted to know if the British were preparing to move. He had received intelligence that General Howe planned to pull the British troops out of Philadelphia and return to New York. Washington soon learned the reports were true.

The next month, the British began their march out of Pennsylvania. On June 18, Washington wrote to Congress with his plans. "I have put six brigades in motion; and the rest of the army are preparing to follow…. We shall proceed towards Jersey.…"

The long stay at Valley Forge was finally over. Now the army was rested, well-trained, and ready for battle. Within days, the Americans met up with the British at Monmouth Courthouse in New Jersey. About 4,000 troops under General Charles Lee began the battle for the Americans. Lee thought he was attacking a small British force. Instead, the main army was closing in on him and his troops. Lee began to retreat, which angered Washington. General Washington rode to the battle lines and took

General Charles Lee

command, keeping the soldiers fighting while the main American army entered the battle.

When the fighting ended, neither side had won a clear victory. The Americans, however, had shown they

George Washington led his troops at the Battle of Monmouth Courthouse.

could battle the main British army and hold their ground.
Steuben's discipline had helped the Americans keep fighting even under the worst conditions.

Monmouth Courthouse was the last major battle of
the American Revolution that was fought in the northern

states. After 1778, the focus shifted to the South, especially the Carolinas and Virginia. The Continental Army would not spend another winter in Pennsylvania.

The time at Valley Forge had been crucial to Washington and his troops. After Valley Forge, few Americans would question Washington's ability to lead. The army was better trained, with a new supply system that worked well. The experience had made the Americans a stronger fighting force. It also showed how much pain and suffering they could stand as they struggled for their independence.

Winter at Valley Forge

GLOSSARY

ammunition—bullets or shells fired out of weapons

casualties— soldiers killed, wounded, captured or missing in battle

civilians—people not part of a military force

commissary—storage place for an army's food and supplies

deserted—left a post in the military without permission

foraging—searching, especially for food

forges—places where iron is heated and shaped into different objects

intelligence—reports sent by spies to their commanders

militias—military forces, often made up of volunteers

nobleman—member of the ruling class

quartermaster—military department or officer in charge of getting supplies to troops

rations—food given to soldiers each day

DID YOU KNOW?

- According to one historian, American troops at Valley Forge played an early form of baseball.

- George Washington chose not to be paid for his service as commander in chief of the Continental Army.

- Martha Washington, the general's wife, spent some time with her husband at Valley Forge.

- Horses also felt the effects of the supply problem at Valley Forge, and many died of starvation.

IMPORTANT DATES

Timeline

1775	The American Revolution begins outside Boston, Massachusetts, on April 19
1777	The British defeat the Continental Army at Brandywine Creek on September 11; the British occupy Philadelphia on September 26; American and British troops clash in Germantown on October 4; Washington sets up camp at Valley Forge on December 19
1778	Severe food shortage at Valley Forge during February; Friedrich von Steuben arrives at Valley Forge on February 23 and begins training the men in March; Nathanael Greene takes over as quartermaster general on March 2; Washington's main army leaves Valley Forge on June 19 and nine days later fights the British at Monmouth Courthouse
1781	The Americans win the Battle of Yorktown, the last major battle of the American Revolution

IMPORTANT PEOPLE

HORATIO GATES (1728–1806)
American general who won the Battle of Saratoga; was considered a possible replacement for George Washington as commander in chief

NATHANAEL GREENE (1742–1786)
General and quartermaster general in the Continental Army; won several key victories in later years of the Revolution

SIR WILLIAM HOWE (1729–1814)
Commander in chief of British forces in North America from 1775 to 1778

THE MARQUIS DE LAFAYETTE (1757–1834)
French nobleman who volunteered to fight for the Americans and served at Valley Forge

CHARLES LEE (1731–1782)
American general who ordered a retreat during the Battle of Monmouth Courthouse

FRIEDRICH VON STEUBEN (1730–1794)
Prussian officer who trained American troops at Valley Forge

GEORGE WASHINGTON (1732–1799)
Commander in chief of the Continental Army during the American Revolution; later served as first president of the United States

WANT TO KNOW MORE?

At the Library

Adelson, Bruce. *Baron von Steuben: American General.* Philadelphia: Chelsea House, 2002.

Bigelow, Barbara, and Linda Schmittroth. *American Revolution: Almanac.* Farmington Hills, Mich.: UXL, 2000.

Burgan, Michael. *George Washington.* Minneapolis: Compass Point Books, 2002.

Dolan, Edward. *The Winter at Valley Forge.* New York: Benchmark Books/Marshall Cavendish, 2002.

Smolinski, Diane. *Revolutionary War Soldiers.* Chicago: Heinemann Library, 2002.

On the Web

For more information on *Valley Forge,* use FactHound to track down Web sites related to this book.

1. Go to *www.compasspointbooks.com/facthound*

2. Type in this book ID: 0756506158

3. Click on the *Fetch It* button.

Your trusty FactHound will fetch the best Web sites for you!

Through the Mail

Valley Forge Convention and Visitors Bureau

600 W. Germantown Pike

Plymouth Meeting, PA 19462

610/834-1550

To get information about visiting the Valley Forge area

On the Road

Valley Forge National Historic Park

North Gulph Road

Valley Forge, PA 19482

610/783-1077

To learn more about the Continental Army's experience at Valley Forge and explore the grounds

INDEX

Barren Hill, 37–38
Battle of Brandywine, 9, 10, *10*
Battle of Germantown, 11–12, *11*
Battle of Monmouth Courthouse, 38, 40, *40*
Battle of Saratoga, 15–16, *15*
Battle of Trenton, 16, *17*
Board of War, 28
Brandywine Creek, 9, 10, *10*
Burgoyne, John, *15*

Commissary Department, 12–13, 31–32
Congress, 6, 12–13, 16, 23, *23*, 24, 25–26, 27–28, 31, 32, 38
Continental Army, 4–6, *4, 5*, 8, *8, 12, 13, 14*, 15, *17, 19, 26*, 31, 34, 35, *36, 40*, 41
Conway, Thomas, 27–28

Delaware River, 14, *17*

foraging missions, 24, 30
Fort Mifflin, 14, *14*
France, 6, 35–37

Gates, Horatio, *15*, 16, 28, *28*
Germantown, Pennsylvania, 11–12, *11*
Greene, Nathanael, 31–32, *31*

Howe, Sir William, 9, *9, 30*, 38

inspector general, 28

Lafayette, Marquis de, *36, 37, 37*
Lee, Charles, 38, *39*
Loyalists, 31

map, *18*
militias, 8, 13
Monmouth Courthouse, 38, 40, *40*

Peale, Charles Willson, *7, 22, 28, 31, 34, 37*
Philadelphia, Pennsylvania, 5, 9, 10, 14, 17, 18, 21, 38
Princeton, New Jersey, 16

Quartermaster Department, 12, 13, 31

Saratoga, New York, 15–16, *15*
Schuylkill River, 19
von Steuben, Friederich, 6, 32–34, *33, 34*, 35
supplies, 5–6, 12, 13, 20, 22–24, 25, 26, 30, 32, 36, 37

training, 34
Trenton, New Jersey, 16, *17*

Valley Forge, *4, 5, 19, 21, 23, 25, 27, 29, 35, 36, 41*
Varnum, James, 22–23, *22*

Wadsworth, Jeremiah, 32
Washington, George, 4, *4*, 5, 6, 7, 8, 10, 11, 12, 15, 16, *17*, 19, 20, *21*, 22, 23, *23*, 24, *25*, 26–27, *27*, 28, 30, 31, 32–33, 35, *36*, 37, 38–39, *40*, 41
Whitemarsh, Pennsylvania, 15, 20

About the Author

Michael Burgan is a freelance writer of books for children and adults. A history graduate of the University of Connecticut, he has written more than 60 fiction and nonfiction children's books for various publishers. For adult audiences, he has written news articles, essays, and plays. Michael Burgan is a recipient of an Educational Press Association of America award and belongs to the Society of Children's Book Writers and Illustrators.